First World War
and Army of Occupation
War Diary
France, Belgium and Germany

27 DIVISION
Divisional Troops
Divisional Signal Company
1 September 1915 - 30 November 1915

WO95/2258/5

The Naval & Military Press Ltd
www.nmarchive.com
Published in association with The National Archives

Published by

The Naval & Military Press Ltd

Unit 10 Ridgewood Industrial Park,

Uckfield, East Sussex,

TN22 5QE England

Tel: +44 (0) 1825 749494

www.naval-military-press.com

www.nmarchive.com

This diary has been reprinted in facsimile from the original. Any imperfections are inevitably reproduced and the quality may fall short of modern type and cartographic standards.

© Crown Copyright
Images reproduced by permission of The National Archives, London, England, 2015.

Contents

Document type	Place/Title	Date From	Date To
Heading	WO95/2258-5		
Heading	27th Divl Signals Coy. Sep-Nov 1915		
Heading	27th Signal Co. R.E. Sep & Oct 15 Vol I.		
Heading	War Diary of 27th Divisional Signal Company R.E. From Sept.1st to Sept. 30th 1915		
War Diary	Croix De Bac	01/09/1915	16/09/1915
War Diary	Merris	16/09/1915	18/09/1915
War Diary	Warfusee-Abencourt	19/09/1915	20/09/1915
War Diary	Mericourt	21/09/1915	30/09/1915
Heading	War Diary of 27th Divisional Signal Company R.E. from 1st Oct to 31st Oct 1915		
War Diary	Mericourt	01/10/1915	26/10/1915
War Diary	Bovelles	27/10/1915	31/10/1915
Heading	War Diary of 27th Divl Sig. Coy From November 1st 1915 to November 30th 1915 Vol II		
War Diary	Bovelles	01/11/1915	30/11/1915

msg/2258(5)

msg/2258(5)

27TH DIVISION
DIVL ENGINEERS

27TH DIVL SIGNAL COY.
SEP - NOV 1915

27th [Brown?]

M 27th Signal Co. R.E.

Sept + Oct - '15

Vol I.

121/74449

Army Form C. 2118.

WAR DIARY
or
INTELLIGENCE SUMMARY.
(Erase heading not required.)

Hour, Date, Place	Summary of Events and Information	Remarks and references to Appendices
	Confidential War Diary of 27th Divisional Signal Company R.E. from Sept. 1st to Sept. 30th 1915	

Instructions regarding War Diaries and Intelligence Summaries are contained in F.S. Regs., Part II and the Staff Manual respectively. Title pages will be prepared in manuscript.

WAR DIARY
OR
INTELLIGENCE SUMMARY.
(Erase heading not required.)

Army Form C. 2118.

Hour, Date, Place	Summary of Events and Information	Remarks and references to Appendices
1 Sept. 1915 CROIX DE BAC	Comic antics said to connect the Three Pigeon Lofts allotted to the Division at BAC St MAUR with the Divisional Signal Office at CROIX DE BAC. All birds good, nothing else to report.	
2/9/15 ditto	Sandbags against wall of Divisional exchange next door to 9th Bde RFA HQs in ARMENTIÈRES collapsed at 6 a.m. no one injured, collapse due to rotten bags at base of wall. Dugouts at Advanced Div. H.Q. ROLANDERIE farm reported complete. Work of wiring signal office Dugouts being mds by Corp. Smith.	
3/9/15 ditto	O.C. goes on leave. 10 men from Div. Cyclist Coy rebuilt collapsed wall of sandbags.	

Army Form C. 2118.

WAR DIARY
or
INTELLIGENCE SUMMARY.
(Erase heading not required.)

Instructions regarding War Diaries and Intelligence Summaries are contained in F. S. Regs., Part II. and the Staff Manual respectively. Title pages will be prepared in manuscript.

Hour, Date, Place	Summary of Events and Information	Remarks and references to Appendices
CROIX DE BAC 3/9/15 (continued)	A. Detachment laid telephone pair to Right Pole Report Centre.	
4/9/15 ditto	A.U. Detachments at work registering and extending lines.	
5/9/15 ditto	nothing to report	
6/9/15 ditto	A. Detachment laid observation line along front trenches for Mountain Battery. Reinforcements :- Sapper Observations :- Driver	

WAR DIARY
or
INTELLIGENCE SUMMARY.
(Erase heading not required.)

Army Form C. 2118.

Hour, Date, Place	Summary of Events and Information	Remarks and references to Appendices
16/9/15 CROIX DE BAC	A Detachment continued work on mountain Battery line. Other Detachments kept working in RIVIÈRE DE LAIE	
8/9/15 ditto	A + C Detachments working on mountain Artillery lines other detachments regulating existing lines. Reinforcements mit Evacuations = 1 Officer	
9/9/15 ditto	A + C Detachments working on mountain Battery lines. Six numbers a b operators attached from 23rd Signal Coy for instruction Reinforcements = 1 Officer.	

Army Form C. 2118.

WAR DIARY
or
INTELLIGENCE SUMMARY.
(Erase heading not required.)

Instructions regarding War Diaries and Intelligence Summaries are contained in F.S. Regs., Part II. and the Staff Manual respectively. Title pages will be prepared in manuscript.

Hour, Date, Place	Summary of Events and Information	Remarks and references to Appendices
10/9/15 CROIX DE BAC	All Detachments regulating and labelling lines. Evacuations 1 pioneer	
11/9/15 ditto	nothing to Report	
12/9/15 ditto	The whole of the 23rd Signal Coy arrived and moved in field adjoining the Signal Office.	
13/9/15 ditto	Decided that Retired Brigade Headquarters shall be shifted as follows. The Right Bde. the move to ROLANDERIE FARM and Left Bde. take over Right Bde. Headquarters. The requisite wires to make the move possible with interrupting communication were laid by the 23rd Signal Coy. Evacuations = 1 Sapper	

WAR DIARY
or
INTELLIGENCE SUMMARY.
(Erase heading not required.)

Army Form C. 2118.

Hour, Date, Place	Summary of Events and Information	Remarks and references to Appendices
14/9/15 CROIX DE BAC	Operations at 8 P.M. and 82nd Brigade HQs were relieved by 23rd Signal Coy. 80th Bde HQ moved from STEENWERCK to STRAZEEL at 7 p.m. 82nd Bde HQ moved to STEENWERCK at same hour on being relieved by the 70th Bde of the 23rd Division.	
15/9/15 ditto	81st Bde HQ moved to STEENWERCK on relief by the 69th Bde of the 23rd Div., 82nd Bde HA moved from STEENWERCK to GRAND SEC BOIS. Reinforcement Sappers & 23rd Div G.O.C. took over command of our front at 10 a.m.	
15/9/15 ditto	Signal Company marched at 10 a.m. for MERRIS and 2 I hunt Gordon T.E. & GOODWIN left at 7 a.m. one return of office staff to take over MERRIS Wire from 23rd Division.	

Army Form C. 2118.

WAR DIARY
or
INTELLIGENCE SUMMARY.
(Erase heading not required.)

Instructions regarding War Diaries and Intelligence Summaries are contained in F.S. Regs., Part II. and the Staff Manual respectively. Title pages will be prepared in manuscript.

Hour, Date, Place	Summary of Events and Information	Remarks and references to Appendices
16/9/15 MERRIS (continued)	Divisional Signal office opened at MERRIS at 10 a.m. no wire exist out. simply telephone and counter to III Corps.	
17/9/15 ditto	81st Inf Bde H.Q. moved at 5.30 a.m. to VIEUX BERQUIN from STEENWERCK. Lieut. GOODWYN left at noon for the new area in the CRA's car. Reinforcements = 1 Bde Section Sergt. 1 Sapper 1 Pioneer 3 Drivers	
18/9/15 ditto	I moved off at 8.15 a.m. with 2nd Lt. Gordon & the whole of No. 1 Section less the following who were left to run the office until all troops had left for the new area:— one D. Detachment	

Army Form C. 2118.

WAR DIARY
or
INTELLIGENCE SUMMARY.
(Erase heading not required.)

Instructions regarding War Diaries and Intelligence Summaries are contained in F. S. Regs., Part II and the Staff Manual respectively. Title pages will be prepared in manuscript.

Hour, Date, Place	Summary of Events and Information	Remarks and references to Appendices
18/9/16 MERRIS (continued)	Details left behind D. Detachment. (Travelled with R.A. Headquarters) 2 Signal Clerks 2 Register clerks 2 Motor cyclists 4 orderlies. Our route was as follows:— Via STRAZEELE & HAZEBROUCK, to THIENNES, arrived there at 3.15 pm. Train left at 8.25 pm, train arrived GUILLAUCOURT 7 am on Septr. 19th. Departures = 1 Corporal to England on Instruction for New Armies.	

(73989) W4141—463. 400,000. 9/14. H.&J.Ltd. Forms/C. 2118/10.

Army Form C. 2118.

WAR DIARY
or
INTELLIGENCE SUMMARY.
(Erase heading not required.)

Instructions regarding War Diaries and Intelligence Summaries are contained in F.S. Regs., Part II. and the Staff Manual respectively. Title pages will be prepared in manuscript.

Hour, Date, Place	Summary of Events and Information	Remarks and references to Appendices
Sept 19, 1915 WARFUSÉE – ABENCOURT	On detraining we marched to WARFUSÉE – ABENCOURT. Officer fund at Temporary Div. H.Q. at noon. Telephone prior to handing to XII Corps at VILLERS BRETONNEUX was the only line.	
20/9/15 ditto	During night 19th/20th 80th Brigade took over portion of front held by left Battalion of 309 French Brigade and 82nd Brigade the portion of front held by left Battalion of Same Brigade. At 9 am I proceeded to CAPPI with Lieutenant Goodwin & met the French Signalling officer. I inspected	

WAR DIARY
or
INTELLIGENCE SUMMARY.
(Erase heading not required.)

Army Form C. 2118.

Hour, Date, Place	Summary of Events and Information	Remarks and references to Appendices
20/4/16 NARFUSÉE- (continued) -ABENCOURT	The French Signal Officer there and afterwards selected building as Signal Office for us at MÉRICOURT. At 3 p.m. I proceeded with the whole of No.1 Section (less 1 relief of office staff left in temporary office) to MÉRICOURT & occupied new billet by lake west of CHATEAU. A & B Detachments under Lieut. GORDON proceeded to MÉRICOURT on afternoon of 19th up to on the 20th. with two Cable Carts to CAPPY. 80th Brigade took over remaining portion of front held by 309th French Brigade	

WAR DIARY
or
INTELLIGENCE SUMMARY.
(Erase heading not required.)

Army Form C. 2118.

Hour, Date, Place	Summary of Events and Information	Remarks and references to Appendices
20/9/15 WARFUSÉE - ABENCOURT (continued)	10pm Forwarded French list of mines for whole of their front (concluding in 2nd Div. Area) to Signals XII Corps. French mines were roughly permanent vaults with some eighty heavy French cable.	
21/9/15 MERICOURT	G.O.C. 27th Div. took over command from the French of the portion of their front held by the 309th Bde at 8 am. We took over communications from French Signal officer at 8 am. Employed Pioneer Detachment laid third cable line to CAPPY	

WAR DIARY
or
INTELLIGENCE SUMMARY.
(Erase heading not required.)

Army Form C. 2118.

Hour, Date, Place	Summary of Events and Information	Remarks and references to Appendices
21/9/15 MERICOURT (continued)	Knicn— The front held by the Division was inadequate during night of 21/22 as follows:— 82nd Bde took over from 80th Bde the front line due EAST of southern corner of BOIS VIERGE to a point in the front line one sector to the known as DOMPIERRE and FRISE sector. The front is now divided into two sectors to the known as DOMPIERRE and FRISE sector. The Boundary between the Brigades is as follows. Southern edge of BOIS VIERGE — BOYAU LANUSSE (which will belong to DOMPIERRE sector) — CAPPRINERCOURT Road as far as orchard (orchard to belong to FRISE sector; thence in westerly direction to the whole of CAPPI belong to FRISE sector	

Army Form C. 2118.

WAR DIARY
or
INTELLIGENCE SUMMARY.
(Erase heading not required.)

Instructions regarding War Diaries and Intelligence Summaries are contained in F. S. Regs., Part II. and the Staff Manual respectively. Title pages will be prepared in manuscript.

Hour, Date, Place		Summary of Events and Information	Remarks and references to Appendices
22/9/15	MERICOURT	Telephone line between 80th & 82nd Brigades was this [day] at 6 a.m. but communication was maintained through the vibrator line until it could be repaired. Inf. Detachments erecting Airline to FROISSY to replace cable.	
23/9/15	ditto	All Detachments erecting Airline to replace Cable lines.	
24/9/15	ditto	Frontage held by 82nd Inf. Bde extended up to & including work running from THIEPVAL to FONTAINE LE CHAPPI. This frontage being taken over from the 67th Brigade of 22nd Div. during the day.	

WAR DIARY
or
INTELLIGENCE SUMMARY.
(Erase heading not required.)

Army Form C. 2118.

Hour, Date, Place	Summary of Events and Information	Remarks and references to Appendices
24/9/15 MERICOURT (continued)	Divisional Boundary will now run from a point Von FAY - FONTAINE LESCAPPY road, south of FONTAINE LESCAPPY and PROYART to a point on the AMIENS-PERONNE road 200 yards west of the PROYART-RAINECOURT road junction. Corps Headquarters moved to CRISSY. 81st Inf. Brigade HQ. moved to PROYART at 2 p.m. 62nd Inf. Brigade HQ. moved to CHIGNOLLES from CAPPY. Reinforcements:- 2 Lt. Gillis arrived at 10 a.m. to replace Lt. Evelyh at 80th Bde. Signals. 1 Sapper	

WAR DIARY
or
INTELLIGENCE SUMMARY.
(Erase heading not required.)

Army Form C. 2118.

Hour, Date, Place	Summary of Events and Information	Remarks and references to Appendices
24/9/15 MERICOURT (continued)	Lt E.N. EVELEGH RE left at 8.45 am on transfer to Signals Indian Cav. Corps EVACUATED:- 1 Sergeant 2 Sappers 1 Driver	
25/9/15 ditto	Detachments all busy replacing cable with airline; weather very wet, nothing else to report. Capt. Rawton RE replaced Major Rutter in command of XII Corps Signals. 3 repeated air Brigade Signal officers.	
26/9/15 ditto	8th Bat Indt. Bde H.Q. moved to PROYART from WARFUSEE-ABENCOURT at 2.30 pm	

WAR DIARY
or
INTELLIGENCE SUMMARY.
(Erase heading not required.)

Army Form C. 2118.

Hour, Date, Place	Summary of Events and Information	Remarks and references to Appendices
26/9/15 MERICOURT (continued)	Reinforcements :— 1 Motor cyclist.	
27/9/15 ditto	All detachments at work on Aitkin Showery miserable day. XII Corps laid wire own to replace French one tric one.	
28/9/15 ditto	Transferred office at 4 pm from old French office in chateau to new office in the grounds. French also now doing works of the canal extended to our HQ. 10th Bde RFA at CERISY Evacuations :— 1 Sapper.	

WAR DIARY
or
INTELLIGENCE SUMMARY.
(Erase heading not required.)

Army Form C. 2118.

Hour, Date, Place	Summary of Events and Information	Remarks and references to Appendices
29/9/15 MERICOURT	Drew the following remounts at MORCOURT at 3 p.m. 3 officers chargers 1 Riden 5 Light Draft. nothing else to report.	
30/9/15 ditto	Inspected event of Chateau at CAPPY with a view to its becoming Advanced Divisional Headquarters. In the afternoon I took the OC 26th Fd. Cgrade round the line & showed him the officers arrangements.	

Army Form C. 2118.

WAR DIARY
or
INTELLIGENCE SUMMARY.
(Erase heading not required.)

Instructions regarding War Diaries and Intelligence Summaries are contained in F.S. Regs., Part II. and the Staff Manual respectively. Title pages will be prepared in manuscript.

Hour, Date, Place	Summary of Events and Information	Remarks and references to Appendices
	Confidential War Diary of # Divisional Signal Company R.E. from 1st Oct to 31st Oct 1915	

WAR DIARY
or
INTELLIGENCE SUMMARY.
(Erase heading not required.)

Army Form C. 2118.

Hour, Date, Place	Summary of Events and Information	Remarks and references to Appendices
1/10/15 MERICOURT	I took 2 Lt Upneyham of 26th Signals round the lines & explained to him my office arrangements. B. Detachment under 2Lt Gordon laid line from Chatam at CAPPY to FONTAINE LES CAPPY. E evacuation :- 1 Sapper 1 Driver A B + C Detachments went out on practice schemes. I inspected all B 2nd Arc lines during the morning & made enquiries re special mining lines. R. Detachment laid River line from ECLUSIER to CAPPY	
2/10/15 ditto		

WAR DIARY
or
INTELLIGENCE SUMMARY.
(Erase heading not required.)

Army Form C. 2118.

Hour, Date, Place	Summary of Events and Information	Remarks and references to Appendices
3/10/15 MERICOURT	A & R detachments having bivouacked continued to take part in Schemes. B. Detachment cont. read in training Court to the dugout on canal bank. A Detachment teach in personnel line with H.Q. Bre. Am. Column. 9 am. excursion of 2nd line to 20th Bde R.F.A.	
4/10/15 ditto	81st Bnf. Ren. relieved 82nd Inf. Bde in Right sector during the day. Visited O.C. 22nd Div. Supply & asked him about the issue of 100 × Bde R.F.A. at CHUIGNE requested.	

Army Form C. 2118.

WAR DIARY
or
INTELLIGENCE SUMMARY.
(Erase heading not required.)

Instructions regarding War Diaries and Intelligence Summaries are contained in F. S. Regs., Part II. and the Staff Manual respectively. Title pages will be prepared in manuscript.

Hour, Date, Place	Summary of Events and Information	Remarks and references to Appendices
4/10/15 MERICOURT (continued)	Laid cable line to Bomb School taking off line to 22nd Div. 1 mile south of MERICOURT. D. Detachment reported 1st Ride RFA Vibrator line ~. Reinforcements = 1 Pioneer	
5/10/15 ditto	A & B detachments cable line to Bomb School with Airline. C + D detachments constructed Airline to CERISY and replaced french cable line to 20th Bde RFA Reinforcement = 1 Sergeant	

(73989) W4141—463. 400,000. 9/14. H.&J.Ltd. Forms/C. 2118/10.

WAR DIARY
or
INTELLIGENCE SUMMARY.
(Erase heading not required.)

Army Form C. 2118.

Hour, Date, Place	Summary of Events and Information	Remarks and references to Appendices
1/10/15 MERICOURT	A detachment laid cable pair from FROISSY to 1st Bde RFA repairing trench cable pair. I visited the left Bde advanced Headquarters with Lt. Ellis, 2nd Lt Gordon with 50 E cyclists dug trench from CAPPY Chateau to the canal for burying wires.	
7/10/15 ditto	A detachment regulating lines between 80th & 82nd Bdes. B C & D Detachments commenced two days practice scheme. Reinforcements = 1 sapper, 1 motor cyclist	

Army Form C. 2118.

WAR DIARY
or
INTELLIGENCE SUMMARY.
(Erase heading not required.)

Instructions regarding War Diaries and Intelligence Summaries are contained in F.S. Regs., Part II. and the Staff Manual respectively. Title pages will be prepared in manuscript.

Hour, Date, Place	Summary of Events and Information	Remarks and references to Appendices
8/10/15 MERICOURT	A. Detachment regulating vibrator line to 80th Inf. Bde. B.C. & A. Detachments continued practice scheme. 80th Bde. telephone wire found to have been divided in BRAY in error, communication maintained through vibrator line. Casualties = 1 Sergeant.	
9/10/15 ditto	All Detachments cleaning wagons, repairing cables, nothing else to report.	

WAR DIARY
or
INTELLIGENCE SUMMARY.
(Erase heading not required.)

Army Form C. 2118.

Instructions regarding War Diaries and Intelligence Summaries are contained in F.S. Regs., Part II. and the Staff Manual respectively. Title pages will be prepared in manuscript.

Hour, Date, Place	Summary of Events and Information	Remarks and references to Appendices
10/10/15 MERICOURT	Interchange of Regiments of the 82nd Bde + 67th Bde begun nothing to report	
11/10/15 ditto	Moves — Royal Irish Fusiliers PROYART & HERBONNIÈRES. R.C.d.I. ABANCOURT to VAUVILLERS. 5th S.W.B. FRAMERVILLE to PROYART 11th Welsh Regt. VAUVILLERS to CAPPY 4th K.R.R. CAPPY to MORCOURT A.T.R. Detachments constructing mining line from CAPPY to DUM PIERRE. c.R.E. Detachments constructing aerodrome from PROISSY to CAPPY	

WAR DIARY or INTELLIGENCE SUMMARY.

Army Form C. 2118.

Hour, Date, Place	Summary of Events and Information	Remarks and references to Appendices
14/10/15 MERICOURT (continued)	to repair permanent line round BRAY for 80 to Bde Telephone line. Sergeant Bentney supersedes Corp. Flinn as commander of 13.A detachment. II Corps Gregson takes Sergt. Bentney's place as signal clerk. Electric light lorry Scott attached to Signal Coy to [...] Clothing + equipment from this date. Reinforcement = 2 Sappers, 1 Pioneer.	

WAR DIARY
or
INTELLIGENCE SUMMARY.

(Erase heading not required.)

Army Form C. 2118.

Instructions regarding War Diaries and Intelligence Summaries are contained in F.S. Regs., Part II. and the Staff Manual respectively. Title pages will be prepared in manuscript.

Hour, Date, Place	Summary of Events and Information	Remarks and references to Appendices
12/10/15 MERICOURT	Movement Ministers to YAVVILLERS Royal Irish Division to ABANCOURT C + A Detachments completed ride upon yesterday.	
13/10/15 ditto	Royal Irish to YAVVILLERS 7th SWB to MOR COURT HQs 82nd Bde to FRAMERVILLE HQs 61st Bde to PROYART A Detachment proceeded at 4.30 pm to lay tin line from Canal to communication trench near advanced left Bde Headquarters	

Army Form C. 2118.

WAR DIARY
or
INTELLIGENCE SUMMARY.
(Erase heading not required.)

Instructions regarding War Diaries and Intelligence Summaries are contained in F.S. Regs., Part II. and the Staff Manual respectively. Title pages will be prepared in manuscript.

Hour, Date,-Place	Summary of Events and Information	Remarks and references to Appendices
13/10/15 MERICOURT (continued)	A. R.E. Detachments regulating line. B Detachment laid wire from Signal office to CRE's office. C Detachment clearing room at Detachment Hd Qrs going. A R E Detachments repairing road to Signal office. D Detachment cutting undergrowth. Nothing else to report Reinforcements = 1 Motor cyclist	
14/10/15 ditto		

WAR DIARY
or
INTELLIGENCE SUMMARY.
(Erase heading not required.)

Army Form C. 2118.

Hour, Date, Place	Summary of Events and Information	Remarks and references to Appendices
15/10/15 MERICOURT	all detachments cleaning harness & wagons. General inspection at 2.30 pm. 4 p.m. A.S.C. detachments started 3rd practice retreat. In the afternoon I visited trenches round the VICRERIE to inspect R.A. lines, with Adjt. 20th Bde R.F.A. Evacuations = 1 Driver. During the day 67th Bde relieved the 80th Bde in left sector. G.O.C. 67th Bde assumed command of sector at 1830. Travelling Company relieved 2nd reserve ammunition company in factory.	
16/10/15 ditto		

WAR DIARY
or
INTELLIGENCE SUMMARY

(Erase heading not required.)

Army Form C. 2118.

Hour, Date, Place	Summary of Events and Information	Remarks and references to Appendices
14/10/15 MERICOURT (continued)	On better fixed by an orderly is attached to the 8th Inf. Bde. 1st Western Force by gone into Reserve at MERICOURT. A.P.C detachments continue practice scheme; R. Detachment begins construction of Airline to 27th Siege Arts HQ at FRAMERVILLE. B. Detachment continues construction of Airline commenced yesterday; return at H.Q.C Detachments upon on completion of Practice Scheme; Both fine through foggy.	
17/10/15	ditto	

WAR DIARY or INTELLIGENCE SUMMARY

Army Form C. 2118.

Hour, Date, Place	Summary of Events and Information	Remarks and references to Appendices
18/10/15 MERICOURT	In morning I inspected Signal Offices at 4th K.R.R., 1st W. Yorks, and 8th Cambridgeshire Regts H.Q. with Signal officers of 67th Bde. 8th Bulldogs constructed airline under Lieut. Ryan to approx. a mile from PERONNE-AMIENS road to PROYART. D. Detachment completed airline to 27th Siege Bde H.Q. B. 10. Detachment regulating airline to FROISSY. A+C Detachments repairing road to Signal office. 17th Corps Detachment arrived on loan to help in construction of lines for Corps artillery.	

WAR DIARY or INTELLIGENCE SUMMARY

Army Form C. 2118.

Hour, Date, Place	Summary of Events and Information	Remarks and references to Appendices
19/10/15 MERICOURT	D. Detachment laid safety line at river from CAPPY to FROISSY. 12th Corps detachments at work on heavy battery lines. 2nd Lieuts Porter, Heyward & Pennney arrived for attachment from the 4/5th Signal Coy. Lt Moorhead RE & 2/12th Corps Detachment arrived at 1 pm & started work on heavy artillery lines. Animals arrived.	
20/10/15 ditto	80th Inf Bde relieved 67th Bde in Left Sector. 67th Bde goes into Divisional Reserve at PROYART. 17th Corps Detachments continue work on Heavy Artillery lines.	

Army Form C. 2118.

WAR DIARY
or
INTELLIGENCE SUMMARY

(Erase heading not required.)

Hour, Date, Place	Summary of Events and Information	Remarks and references to Appendices

21/10/18 MERICOURT 67th Inf. Bde. moved out of PROYART at 9 am to rejoin the 23rd Division. 15th Corps Detachments left at 8.30 am to M - Detachment rued up line to Advanced left Bde H.Q. A Detachment rued up cater which had previously been replaced by Airline by 80th Inf. Bde Signal Section. B. Detachment rued up cable line FROISY to CAPPY. Evacuations = 1 strain 1 supper

WAR DIARY
or
INTELLIGENCE SUMMARY

Army Form C. 2118.

Hour, Date, Place	Summary of Events and Information	Remarks and references to Appendices
20/10/15 MERICOURT	A. Detachment rode up canal bank between CAPPY & the Abgout at CAPPY. Running Detachments overhauling wagons. Mounted Inspection at 2.30 p.m. Lt. ANDERSON R.E. orders to be attached from Tyne Electrical R.E. Evacuation 1 Lance Corporal. 82nd Inf. Bde moved at ABBEN COURT during the afternoon on return from Flaucourt to 22nd Division. Turned over under Command of GOC Xth Corps at 8 a.m. I visited Signalling Officer at GUILLACOURT to meet Lieutenant during the afternoon. Reinforcements = 2 Drivers.	
23/10/15 ditto		

WAR DIARY
or
INTELLIGENCE SUMMARY.
(Erase heading not required.)

Army Form C. 2118.

Instructions regarding War Diaries and Intelligence Summaries are contained in F. S. Regs., Part II and the Staff Manual respectively. Title pages will be prepared in manuscript.

Hour, Date, Place	Summary of Events and Information	Remarks and references to Appendices
24/10/15 MERICOURT	One of the Regiments of the 12th French Brigade relieved the 8/17th Inf Bde in the right sector during the day	
25/10/15 ditto	The remaining Regiment of the 12th French Brigade moved to PROYART. The French Regiment from PROYART relieved the 80th Inf Bde during the evening. The Brigadier of the 12th Brigade took over the Command of our front with GOC 27th Division at 10 a.m. with Headquarters at CAPPY, arranged to have French & English I of portion at both ends of the line until the relief was complete.	

Army Form C. 2118.

WAR DIARY
or
INTELLIGENCE SUMMARY.
(Erase heading not required.)

Hour, Date, Place	Summary of Events and Information	Remarks and references to Appendices
25/10/15 MERICOURT (continued)	The French Division arrived in this afternoon & fitted into their instruments. I sent Lt. Anderton with our relief of operators & cyclist orderlies to the Loevy to BOVELLES new Divisional Office. Reinforcements = 1 Driver. Evacuations = 1 Sapper, 1 Driver.	
26/10/15 ditto	G.O.C. 6th French Division took over command of our front (in addition to that of 22nd Div.) France taken over (by him) at 9 a.m. and the communications of the Division were taken over by the French before start (?) at that hour.	

(73989) W4141—463. 400,000. 9/14. H.&J.Ltd. Forms/C. 2118/10.

WAR DIARY
or
INTELLIGENCE SUMMARY.

(Erase heading not required.)

Army Form C. 2118.

Hour, Date, Place	Summary of Events and Information	Remarks and references to Appendices
26/9/18 MERICOURT (continued)	The Divisional HQ opened at BOYELLES at same hour (9 am) Reconnaissance of cable detachments & Headquarters wagons set out in column of route for BOYES under 2nd Lieut Gordon & Pister at 9 a.m. all others moved under 1st Lieut. Gregson arrived at 9 am for BOYELLES. The lorry brought in the last relief from the Signal Office, I reached BOYELLES in the Lignie car at 11.30 a.m.	

WAR DIARY or INTELLIGENCE SUMMARY.

Army Form C. 2118.

Hour, Date, Place	Summary of Events and Information	Remarks and references to Appendices
2/11/15 BOYELLES	The Detachments & Hd. wagons arrived at 2 p.m. from BOVES. No time to Brigades. All communications done by D.R. Telephone line with supering posted trouble are the only lines, outside the village. Telephone lines laid to Generals Chateau, g. Office & a. officer. B.R runs arranged as follows to all Brigades. 10 a.m. 3 p.m. 6 p.m.	

WAR DIARY
or
INTELLIGENCE SUMMARY.
(Erase heading not required.)

Army Form C. 2118.

Hour, Date, Place	Summary of Events and Information	Remarks and references to Appendices
27/10/15 BOYELLES (continued)	80th Bde Headquarters moved at FERRIÈRES 81st Bde Hqrs. at SEUX 82nd Bde Hqrs. at BUSSY 2 Lt Ellis goes on leave	
28/10/15 ditto	nothing to report Division at rest.	
29/10/15 ditto	nothing to report	
30/10/15 ditto	Conference held at Hqr RA at GUINEMICOURT. Capt Hall goes on leave	
31/10/15 ditto	nothing to report	

Army Form C. 2118.

WAR DIARY
or
INTELLIGENCE SUMMARY.
(Erase heading not required.)

Instructions regarding War Diaries and Intelligence Summaries are contained in F.S. Regs., Part II. and the Staff Manual respectively. Title pages will be prepared in manuscript.

Hour, Date, Place	Summary of Events and Information	Remarks and references to Appendices
	Confidential	12/7663
	War Diary of 27th Divl Sig. Coy	
	from November 1st 1915	
	to November 30th 1915	
	Vol II	

(73989) W4141—463. 400,000. 9/14. H.&J.Ltd. Forms/C. 2118/10.

WAR DIARY
or
INTELLIGENCE SUMMARY.
(Erase heading not required.)

Army Form C. 2118.

Hour, Date, Place	Summary of Events and Information	Remarks and references to Appendices
1/11/15 BOYENES	D. Detachment constructed airline to replace cable line to R.A. Hrs at GUINEMICOURT. Signal Clerks started under Corp. ATE.	
2/11/15 ditto	Lieut. Vinney 81st Bde Signals goes on leave. D. Detachment picked up cable line to R.A. A. Detachment laid cable line from SEVX to BUSSY (from Hd 81st Bde to Hd 82nd Bde) C. Detachment constructed airline a 81st Bde Hrs at SEVX. B. A. T. laid cable to 80th Bde at PERRIERES.	

WAR DIARY
or
INTELLIGENCE SUMMARY.
(Erase heading not required.)

Army Form C. 2118.

Instructions regarding War Diaries and Intelligence Summaries are contained in F.S. Regs., Part II. and the Staff Manual respectively. Title pages will be prepared in manuscript.

Hour, Date, Place	Summary of Events and Information	Remarks and references to Appendices
3/11/15 BOVELLES	A. Detachment replaced cable with Connie airline along permanent route through FLUY towards BUSSY. D. Detachment also worked on farm line; B.Y.C. Detachments cut poles for Connie airline.	
4/11/15 ditto	D. Detachment continue work on airline to BUSSY. A.G. Section continued work on line from BUSSY and and worked until it met D. Detachment, line through at 5 p.m. B. Detachment erected Connie airline to FERRIÈRES to replace cable, line through at 3.30 p.m.	

WAR DIARY
or
INTELLIGENCE SUMMARY.

Army Form C. 2118.

Hour, Date, Place	Summary of Events and Information	Remarks and references to Appendices
5/11/15 BAYELLES	Lt goes on leave till the 9th Nov. Lt Godwin acting OC. Came down to BUSSY Picked up One LD & 6 chargers ammn. one pair H.D. replaced by 2 pair of mules.	
6/11/15 ditto	} nothing to Report.	
7/11/15 ditto		
8/11/15 ditto		
9/11/15 ditto		
10/11/15 ditto		

Army Form C. 2118.

WAR DIARY
or
INTELLIGENCE SUMMARY.
(Erase heading not required.)

Hour, Date, Place	Summary of Events and Information	Remarks and references to Appendices

11/11/15 BOVELLES   Sb L.D. horses returned to Div.
                    train, also 4 riding returned in error,
                    12 mules drawn to replace
                    them.

12/11/15 ditto   24 Riders drawn also 2 to replace
                    those returned in error yesterday.
                    Letter received to say that the following
                    officers will accompany the company
                    additional to the establishment

                    2 — Lieut Pictor
                    2 — Lieut Browning
                    2 — Lieut Hayward

Army Form C. 2118.

WAR DIARY
or
INTELLIGENCE SUMMARY.
(Erase heading not required.)

Hour, Date, Place	Summary of Events and Information	Remarks and references to Appendices
1/11/15 (Continued)	Following Promotions made to complete new Establishment.	
	Corp. Buckingham from Sergt. Complete	
	I Corp. Hitch Corp. vice Colwill 16/9/15	
	II Corp. Hawkridge Corp. vice Buckingham 1/11/15	
	II Corp. Rumbler to complete 1/11/15	
	I Corp. Conein II Corp. vice Hitch 18/9/15	
	II Corp. Cuthbage acting II Corp. vice Hawkridge 1/11/15	
	Dr. Ridpath act. L/Corp. vice Conein 16/9/15	
	Sap. Edmunds L/Corp. vice Cuthage 1/11/15	
	— Buckingham L/Corp. complete 1/11/15	
	— Sullivan act. L/Corp. — 1/11/15	
	— Harrow aft. L/Corp. — 1/11/15	
	— Hughes off. L/Corp. — 1/11/15	
	2nd C/S Gibson to S+C/S Corp. 1/11/15	

WAR DIARY
or
INTELLIGENCE SUMMARY.
(Erase heading not required.)

Army Form C. 2118.

Hour, Date, Place	Summary of Events and Information	Remarks and references to Appendices
13/11/15 ROVELLES	16 mules drawn from Sup. Train for it limbered RE wagon also the other. changed 6 mules from W.1. section " 3 " " " 3 " " 4 " found the necessitates :- Reinforcements :- Corp. F. Dunn & limbered RE's drawn from Railhead (AILLY)	
14/11/15 ditto	nothing to report.	
15/11/15 ditto	8th Bde Sig office closed at 10 am & " " " opened at 8th Pole " " at 10.20 am to meet 80th Bde. on FERRIÈRES at ? Ram. copp.line clrs from 11.50 am to 5.25 pm	

WAR DIARY
or
INTELLIGENCE SUMMARY.
(Erase heading not required.)

Army Form C. 2118.

Hour, Date, Place	Summary of Events and Information	Remarks and references to Appendices
17/11/15 BOVELLES	Reinforcements :- 28 Drivers from Base Depôt.	
18/11/15 ditto	Dr Gardner and Pr Proctor & Proper transferred to A.C. entre section moving the report.	
19/11/15 ditto	All 4 Bdes R.A. connected with telephone :- 10V Pde RFA FERRIÈRES 19th Bde - SEUX 20th Pde - BRIAMESNIL 129th Bde (How) HILLY SUR SOMME nothing to Report	
20/11/15 ditto		

WAR DIARY
or
INTELLIGENCE SUMMARY.
(Erase heading not required.)

Army Form C. 2118.

Hour, Date, Place	Summary of Events and Information	Remarks and references to Appendices
21/11/15 BOVELLES	nothing to report	
22/11/15 ditto	ditto	
23/11/15 ditto	2 mules presented to the mobile vet. with mud fever all remaining mules treated with anti-frostbite.	
24/11/15 ditto	82nd Bde Sig Office closed at BUSSY at 3.40 a.m. 8th Div. Hd.qrs Sig office closed at FERRIÈRES at 7.15 a.m. 8nd Bde Sig. Office opened at FERRIÈRES at 8.20 a.m. circular 7.10 P.m.	

Army Form C. 2118.

WAR DIARY
or
INTELLIGENCE SUMMARY.

(Erase heading not required.)

Instructions regarding War Diaries and Intelligence Summaries are contained in F.S. Regs., Part II. and the Staff Manual respectively. Title pages will be prepared in manuscript.

Hour, Date, Place	Summary of Events and Information	Remarks and references to Appendices
25/11/15 BOYELLES	nothing to report	
26/11/15 ditto		
27/11/15 ditto		
28/11/15 ditto		
29/11/15 ditto		
30/11/15 ditto		
1/12/15 ditto	1st Bar RFA moved to PISSY except twelve specim 15th new 19th Bde RFA of fire element	

www.ingramcontent.com/pod-product-compliance
Lightning Source LLC
Chambersburg PA
CBHW081454160426
43193CB00013B/2482